Casting Vision:
The Power of Seeing
Before You See It

by

Charity A. Morris

Casting Vision:

The Power of Seeing Before You See It

Charity Morris

Casting Vision: The Power of Seeing Before You See It

Copyright 2025 © Charity A. Morris

Published by
Scribe Publications, Inc.
(404) 647-1347
www.scribepublicationsinc.com

ISBN-13: 979-8-9853854-8-9

Printed in the United States of America

Dedication

This book is dedicated to my children, Hebron the Great and Baby Queen Hannah!. At such a young age, you recognie the greatness that is within you. May the light of your confidence never go dim. I love you eternally.

Acknowledgements

Lord I thank YOU! You keep me dreaming BIG! And to my true love, Gary. The support you give needs to be studied. You're at every event, helping with every meeting, and praying for me. Thank you seems too light. I appreciate you!

Table of Contents

Foreword

The last ten plus years of my life have been significantly impacted by the author, Charity Morris. I have watched her grow and develop into a major asset at every Fortune 500 company for which she has worked. Her ability to grow teams, develop skillsets and empower change has made her impact immeasurable.

Outside the corporate culture, Charity's desire to serve the One and Only God through her Lord Jesus Christ has been her shinning character trait. She has studied the Word of God to mold her position as wife, mother, sister and daughter. She uses her solid foundation and stern faith to help develop those who the world has robbed, beaten and broken in pieces to grow their faith and vision to move past their pain. I have never met someone fueled by so much faith and focus to change and impact the world around her. I had to have her as my friend and future.

As you read through these chapters, you will see how much detail has been put into showing each one of us how to visualize our future and take the steps to make things happen. Success comes through panning and planning from an idea. In life, sometimes we need someone who can show us how to make our ideas come to fruition and press toward the mark God has called us all to reach.

Every one of us has a path to take. God gives the direction and also puts people in places along the route to help us achieve what he has for us. David had a Samuel, Lot had Abram, and Joshua had Moses. Each had someone to give them some direction to get where God wanted them. Thank God I have a Charity Morris helping me as I lead as a Pastor, Law Enforcement officer and father.

Please take the time to seek the scriptures and biblically based steps in this book to help you grow to greatness. Be Blessed.

Thanks for stepping out on faith, my love.

Your Husbae,

Pastor G. (Gary Morris)

"To set goals that will inspire you to follow through, you need to create a vision that is so powerful, it captivates you every single day."

~ Ana McRae

Preface

My first experience with creating a vision board was with a lady that I'd met in 2005. She <u>REALLY </u>made me uncomfortable because her commanding presence and uncanny ability to provoke me to dig deeper challenged the insecure little girl that had held me hostage for so many years. This woman pulled me into the deep and helped me to face an imposter syndrome. For the first time in my life, I felt worthy of receiving love and much more because it was coming from a pure place of wanting to be my best so that I can, in turn, help others. Sure, I had said things like 'I love me' and 'I deserve the best,' but it was all a superficial front. Deep down, I was not completely convinced until that destined day.

Today, that purpose pusher and dream doula has become a close confidant and dear friend that I treasure for life. God used my good sis, Yvette Gauff, to stir up dormant gifts as well as cultivate a passion and ravenous appetite to dream BIG, with my eyes and heart wide open. Little did I know that this board would not only be the first of many but would become the catalyst to pursue my purpose in helping others. The residuals from our meeting will last a lifetime and span the globe.

Now, had I heard of vision boards? ABSOLUTELY! With the numerous celebrities and self-help gurus creating these boards, it was difficult to ignore it. Yet me being one who didn't like to follow trends and jump on anyone's bandwagon, I ignored it as just another fad that would soon phase out. Boy was I wrong, and I am so thankful that this was one trend in which I took part.

My first board was a random a total mind mosh pit… an amalgamation of pictures and phrases that represented my thoughts, dreams, and goals. There was certainly no particular order, just massive brain dump. Overtime, I learned the art of refinement so that now my vision boards and life plans have a cohesive flow and focus on specific goals. The sense of accomplishment will never get old as I cross off the goal when it's accomplished. The time, care, attention, intention and discipline it takes to do the work makes the triumph that much sweeter.

From marathons, marriage, motherhood, and mission trips to opening businesses, earning my Six Sigma Black Belt, getting my dream truck and dream house, the vision boards over the years were the foundational tool that helped me cast vision for my life. All of it didn't happen within a year, or two years, or even ten years. But as I kept working the plan, things were getting checked off the boards. In my process, I cried, doubted, walked away, quit, started again, retreated again, but came back because I remembered the commitment I had made to myself in 2005, so I kept pressing forward.

That fateful vision boarding session from January 2005 stirred the visionary goal getter in me. The sleeping giant with an entrepreneurial spirit was now awake, which eventually would lead to me facilitating vision board sessions, vision workshops, and coaching sessions worldwide. I had no idea that our chance meeting followed by an invite to join her two-hour workshop would change my life and have such an impact on others that I now encounter. Whether it's a business consultation, a book publishing workshop, a design session, or a strategic roapmapping meeting with a client, I will always check their vision and belief system. Without a strong vision for the future, our sessions will not be the most beneficial. Once a clear vision is established, then we could move forward in purpose.

Introduction

New year, new hopes, new you!

For some, the closing of one year and the embarkment upon a new year causes them to do a self-evaluation and set lofty goals and resolutions for the year. For others, a pivotal change in life has occurred and is forcing you to figure out what makes you happy. The loss of a loved one, marriage, divorce, birth of a child, job loss, menopause, mid-life crisis are just a few life events that can cause you to pause and reflect. Maybe it's a milestone birthday.... Turning 21, entering the Dirty 30s, hitting the Fabulous 50s, or walking into the Unbothered 60s. Whatever the event, you are here and now's a good time to recess and reassess to decide if your life is heading in the right direction.

Embedded in each of us is a desire to do more, have more, be more. We all have an innate yearning for growth. The desire can move us into a FIGHT, FLIGHT, OR FREEZE mode. It pushes some into greatness, frightens others to retreat to a comfort zone or paralyzes a few, who end up not making a move in any direction.

Because you are reading this book, I choose to believe your desires are pushing you to set new goals and become a better version of yourself. It's compelling you to fulfill that longing to do more. It's directing you beyond talking about it for years to putting a plan in place and then executing it. Regardless of the setbacks and stopping in times past, you're determined to keep going this time.

Sure, you may have set goals but never reached them, which led to becoming less and less motivated but today's a new day. You're turning over a new leaf; you are doing something different for a better life! The something different this time around is planning for your success. You will not only focus on the vision and the goal but also building a path to accomplish the plan.

Before you decide exactly WHAT your goal is, you need to take some time to reflect on how you've been showing up in each area of your life. What has gone well in the past year, two years, five years? What could be improved in the following year?

Some of you don't have a better life because you can't see yourself having a better life. Some may feel like you are not worthy of having more, doing more, being more. Some of you have lost faith in yourself. Some of you have lost faith in God. Some of you have lost the ability to simply believe again. Some of you have more confidence in what won't happen instead of the possibility of what could happen. Disappointment has diminished your ability to dream.

But today's the day that you perform a check-up from the neck up. It's time that you examine how you think, how you perceive, how you believe, which affects what you see. You no longer have the luxury of letting things happen the way they happen. If what you hear, see, and ultimately believe help to shape what you have, could it be, if your believing is off, your receiving can be minimized? Think about it.

It's no secret or surprise that culture can be a major subliminal influence in what we see, hear, and believe. After all, the phrase "fake news" has dominated many news cycles, think pieces, as well as public and private conversations. Although this phrase has be misused and abused in most instances, allow me the liberty to say that some of you have been allowing fake news to permeate your mind. During times when you should have been pushing yourself to move forward and pursue better, the cultural colloquialisms of:

Give yourself grace

Protect your peace

If it doesn't serve me well, then it's got to go

gave you an easy way out. Let's agree to temporarily pause these phrases because they excused you from putting the work in to address the issues at hand. These catchphrases, at first thought, seem innocent and even empowering, but there's a subset of society who has been kept in a serious chokehold and because of these word, gave you license to be complacent, license to be mediocre, license to not challenge yourself, license to not push yourself to be your best.

No longer are you entitled to say, "Well, this is just me." If it's not the BEST authentic you, then it's time to change. When you extend so much grace to yourself that it excuses you from not presenting your best self, to not go after the next level, then it's time to pause and ponder. Explaining it does not excuse it. Push past the comfort zone and go after more…there is more that you can be doing with your gifts, skills, talents, knowledge, and time.

So then how can you shake yourself lose from this sunken space? It starts with these three words. **FIX YOUR FOCUS**. What are you seeing for yourself? Not just with your natural eyes but also with the eyes of your mind. What visions of your future is your mind projecting?

If the vision of yourself is poor, then you will not see a better life for yourself. Just as poor vision with your physical eyes can increase the risk of falls and accidents, injuries due to reduced depth perception, the inability to detect hazards, difficulty navigating environments, so too can poor mental vision can cause depression and anxiety, feelings of frustration, helplessness, isolation, and can undermine healthy self-esteem and confidence. That lack of confidence can cause you to miss career opportunities, promotions, or job retention.

Addressing vision impairment through early detection and corrective measures is crucial to mitigating these negative effects. Having a clear, positive mental image for your life is a powerful tool to aid in personal growth, success, and overall life fulfillment. It's a motivating force that provides clarity, direction, and resilience, helping you stay committed and overcome setbacks and stumbling blocks _when_ they do arise. It becomes easier to prioritize tasks and allocate time to what's most important.

A compelling vision pushes you to take consistent action, even when facing obstacles. When challenges arise, your clear vision reminds you of the bigger picture your mind has shown you. A clear vision allows you to articulate your goals and values to others.

Casting vision effectively is essential for inspiring and motivating others, whether in personal life, leadership, or organizational contexts. It involves clearly communicating your vision, aligning it with shared values, and creating a path for others to engage with and support it. Casting vision is about more than just stating goals; it's about inspiring belief, fostering collaboration, and empowering action toward a shared future. When done effectively, it can transform individuals, teams, and organizations.

Chapter 1

Purpose Pusher

From Simon Sinek's *Find Your Why*, Eric Thomas' *You Owe You*, to Charity Morris' *Casting Vision* (why not, you're reading it now, aren't you!), people of prominence and influence are pushing you to dig deeper to discover the drivers in your life. They... no WE want you to unearth your motivation and reasons of why you do what you do.

What drives you?	What is your motivation?
What inspires you?	What is your end game?
What motivates you?	What were you put on Earth to do?
What angers you?	What comes easy to you?
What excites you?	What are you skilled at doing?
What worries you?	What are your talents?
What stresses you?	Who do you love to help?

What is that thing that keeps you going and gives you purpose?

Why are you sacrificing to get what you want/need?

Before you can dive into creating your vision board to cast a compelling vision, I want you to spend deliberate time reflecting and soul searching. If you don't assess why you are at where you are at this moment in time and where you are going, it will be quite difficult to identify who you wish to become and where you desire to be in the future.

So, before you search for inspiration on Pinterest, before you cut one magazine, before you place one sticker on that board, let's take a beat, a pause, if you will. Put the scissors down, drop the tape and walk away from the board!

The idea of finding your "why" pertains to recognizing your primary purpose, inspiration, or reason for existing. It's the driving force behind your actions, decisions, and goals. Your "why" aligns with your values and passions, serving as a foundation for how you live your life and contribute to the world.

The importance behind your "why" can help give clarity, motivation, alignment, and impact. A strong understanding of your purpose enables you to provide effective contributions to your life, others and ultimately make a difference in society. It serves as a guidepost and influences your life, including career decisions, relationship choices and daily habits.

It's no surprise that most of society wants more, whether it's a better job, more money, a better relationship, better health, more time, more vacations, or just more peace, spiritual growth and happiness. BUT WHY? Why do you want more money? Why do you want to be out of debt? Why do you want a better job? Why do you want more peace, love and happiness? Discovering your "why" is mission critical to help find your focus and target your energy. Having a passionate and purposeful "why" keeps you connected to the appropriate actions. Locking your "why" in the forefront of your mind and eye's view (you guessed it, your vision board) helps you remain steadfast during rough times and uncertain moments. With you "whys" in place, you can more readily make a quality choice of furloughing that trip to Japan in lieu of putting that money towards paying down your credit card debt. You can even turn down a job offer when it doesn't align to your values and purpose. If your goal is sobriety, why take a job at a brewing manufacturing plant, even if it's a $50,000 bump in your salary.

Having a rock-solid "WHY" is the foundation of success. Making more money, having a nice house, getting the hot new car, getting that dream body are merely scratching the surface. To build a strong "why," consider what's most valuable to you, what gives you meaning; the "whys" give you purpose and that purpose will spark your mission in life. The goal is to find a mission for your mindset. Your "why" could be as authentic as leaving a legacy for your children, as ambitious as starting a law practice to help the disenfranchised and underrepresented, as grand as helping people be their best in life, career and business, as intimate as being financially free to care for your aging parents, as noble as being a stay-at-home mom or as impressive as providing clean water to the residents of Haiti. Whatever it is, your "WHY," more than likely, will be BIGGER THAN YOU. When your mission transcends making money or obtaining things, it becomes a powerful driver.

With discovering your "why" comes the responsibility to educate yourself, open your mind, and expand beyond your comfort zone. It's great to leverage feedback from trusted people in your circle, but their voice shouldn't be the lone voice in your journey to discovering "YOU." Theirs should supplement and support YOURS! And while you may share your thoughts and dreams with others, don't expect everyone to understand or agree with your "why." Become settled and find affirmation within yourself.

Some of my "whys" include creating a secure financial future that spans three generations, helping others live in their true purpose and calling, and enjoying the beauty of this world through traveling with family and friends. With my "whys" in place, I am steadily moving towards growing my portfolio so that I am financially enabled to retire at-will or pursue the career I want without being pressured by earning a set salary each year.

While this process may initially challenge your thinking and believing, it is also quite rewarding, as it leads to greater self-awareness, motivation, and satisfaction. This groundwork is empowering you to not only survive but to thrive and live fully, intentionally and unapologetically.

This is not a one and done activity. Just as you tend to evolve over time, so too will the results of this 'discovery,' thus the need to repeat it as you notice changes in your habits and behaviors. Remember, this is a fluid, ever evolving process, so it will flex with you.

Be forewarned, the work you're about to do may not be easy; taking introspective inventory of all the aspects of your life can tempt you to bury your head in the sand. Whether it's rough, rugged and raw or easy like Sunday morning, be vulnerable and transparent with yourself. You owe it to yourself to peel back the layers and rediscover YOU so that nothing and no one, including YOU (sometimes the biggest critic, harshest hater, and worst enemy is YOU!) will be able to hinder you from living your best life.

TAKE ACTION

To list your "whys," carefully read, think about, then answer the below-listed questions and statements, as these will become the basis for your vision board. Continue to ask yourself why it matters repeatedly with each answer to help you drill down until you reach a fundamental, emotional truth and discover the deeper reasons behind your current state and future goals and desires.

1. **Reflect on Your Current Life.** Take stock of your personal, professional, and social life. Identify areas where you feel fulfilled and areas needing improvement.

2. **Reflect on Your Values and Passions**. Your values are the moral bedrock that support who you are and what matters most to you.

Pinpoint Guiding Principles: Ask yourself what core values and ideologies are essential to your existence, what matters most to you (e.g., authenticity, achievements, integrity, balance, faith, compassion, respect).

Ask yourself:

- What do I stand for?
- What qualities do I admire in others?
- What are the principles I would never compromise on? What are my non-negotiables?
- What activities, causes, or ideas make me feel alive and energized? What am I you deeply curious about or drawn to explore further? Look for Patterns: Identify recurring themes in what excites or inspires you.
- What brings me joy? What do I enjoy spending my time doing? Consider hobbies, subjects, or activities you naturally gravitate toward.
- When did I feel the most fulfilled? What was I doing and why did it resonate with me? Think about moments in your life when you felt happiest.
- What legacy do I want to leave for my family? My business? My friends? My community?
- Who do I want to help?
- What problems do I want to solve?

3. Understand Your Strengths

Identify your strengths: Reflect on what you're naturally good at in both a professional and personal setting. What do people thank you for or ask your help to do?

Assess Your Skills: Identify your talents, abilities, and skills you've acquired, including certifications, degrees, trades, workshops attended.

Seek Feedback: Ask trusted friends, colleagues, or mentors what they see as your unique strengths, contributions, talents, skills, and how have you made a difference. Recognize Patterns: Look for recurring themes in your life where your strengths have made a positive impact.

4. Explore Your Life Experiences

Grow from Challenges: Reflect on obstacles or hardships you overcame and list them (they may reveal a deeper calling or give insight into how you can help others facing similar struggles). What happened? How did you feel going through that situation? How did it affect those around you? How did you get through the situation? What were the lessons learned? Consider how past struggles or hardships have shaped your values and aspirations.

5. Define What Fulfillment Means to You

Visualize Your Ideal Life: Imagine what a meaningful, purposeful life looks like to you in one year, three years, five years, ten years. What do success, happiness, and fulfillment look like to you? What would you be doing? Who would be with you? How would you feel? Where would you be?

Identify the "Why" Behind Your Ideal Life: Go beyond surface-level goals to understand the deeper motivations behind why you want what you want.

6. Develop Your "Why" / Purpose Statement. Once you've reflected on your values, passions, strengths, and past experiences, create a statement that defines your "why." Write a short, inspirational statement that depicts your purpose and what you want to attain.

Examples:

"My why is to inspire others to unlock their potential and live authentically."

"I desire to become a life coach to help empower others to achieve their dreams."

"My why in earning my PhD in Family Counseling is so that I can help families who have been affected by parents being in the penal system."

"My why for becoming a comedian is to help heal people through laughter."

"My why is to provide love, support, and stability for my family."

7. Seek Inspiration and Guidance

Read and Learn: Make a list of workshops you can attend, articles and books you can read, podcasts and speeches (i.e. Ted Talks) to help provide insights and spark ideas about purpose and personal growth .

Find Role Models: Study the lives of people you admire as well as those you don't initially know to understand their journey to success and fulfillment. List out what you admire? Do you possess those traits, skills, resolve?

8. **Engage in Self-Discovery Practices:** Journaling, prayer, meditation, or therapy can help you uncover your true desires and intentions. Write about your thoughts, dreams, and feelings to uncover patterns and insights.

9. Take Action and Experiment

Begin exploring activities, projects, or volunteer opportunities that align with your interests and values. You will soon begin to better understand what resonates with you.

10. Connect with a Community

Surround Yourself with Like-Minded People: Join groups or communities that share your passions or goals. If you are unable to find the right fit for you, maybe, just maybe, that's a sign for you to start your own group (THIS HAS BEEN ANOTHER PURPOSE PUSHER MOMENT!). Engaging with others who share similar values can reinforce your sense of purpose.

Be patient and kind to yourself (but don't excuse yourself from doing the work; take a brief break if needed and come back to working on you). Finding your "why" is a journey, not a one-time event or destination. Allow yourself the time, grace and space to grow into it. Your purpose may shift as you gain new experiences or enter different life stages. Continuously seek opportunities for learning and growth to deepen your sense of purpose.

It is up to you to take control of your dreams. Be the gate keeper of your vision. You are officially responsible for your happiness and the manager of your freedom. Begin to identify what living life in purpose, with purpose and on purpose looks like for you, and then build a road map to do just that. You will begin to see that you feel energized and motivated by your daily activities, your work and relationships feel significant and aligned with your values, you experience a greater connection to others and the world, you wake up with a clear sense of direction and enthusiasm, and you experience a sense of fulfillment and joy, even in challenges, which will feel purposeful, not just burdensome.

Chapter 2

The Science Behind Seeing

Why are vision boards so effective in a world where distractions abound? It's not just because they are visually appealing or serve as daily reminders. Vision boards are, in fact, rooted in neuroscience. The secret sauce behind vision boards lies in their capacity to renovate your brains, encourage long-term enthusiasm, and direct you toward your objectives.

Allow me the privilege to geek out for a moment. I was a Biology major in college and the brain has always fascinated me. Embedded in your brain is something called the **Reticular Activating System,** or RAS for short. The RAS behaves as a filter, creating a pecking order of information based on the goals you set. By consistently subjecting yourself to images of your desired outcomes on a vision board, you send bat signals to the RAS to be more keenly aware of opportunities that align with those goals. Is that not mind blowing?

According to renowned neuroscientist Dr. Tara Swart[1]: "Consistently exposing your eye gate to pictures posted on a vision board increases the brain's cognitive ability to recognize and embrace opportunities that may have otherwise been concealed to the mind's eye. This can be explained by the process called value-tagging. Simply put, value tagging engraves significant objects onto your subconscious and filters out unnecessary information." In essence, it helps the brain prioritize information and guides actions. Within milliseconds of seeing it, the brain's visual cortex assigns value to the image; higher value is given to images than to written words.

She further shares "So the more you look at those images, the more those images move up in importance."

The limbic system then adds an emotional layer by tagging things as pleasant and unpleasant. The prefrontal cortex takes into consideration context, goals and prior rewards to further refine the tag. To enhance this activity, it is recommended that you look at your board right before falling asleep (hypnagogia). With each night this is done, the images will be further etched in your brain. That's because the brain is highly sensitive as it falls asleep. So, if you focus your attention on something during that period — particularly on something new — those images are more likely going to be featured in your dreams and thoughts. Once the images have been embedded in your psyche, Swart says, they act as a visual directory and your brain will start to filter out data that is not relevant to them[3].

The act of visualizing a goal can be nearly as powerful as the experience of completing the goal itself. Business psychologist Frank Niles PhD further explains it. "When we visualize a certain behavior, the brain is stimulated to produce an impulse that tells our neurons to 'perform' the movement. This creates a new neural pathway—clusters of cells in our brain that work together to create memories or learned behaviors—that primes our body to act in a way consistent with what we imagined. This occurs without actually performing physical activity, yet it achieves a similar result. This process, known as neuroplasticity, demonstrates how vision boards can influence your brain's wiring and behavior patterns."[4]

Vision boards also have profound psychological benefits. Visualization methodologies have been known to enhance motivation and confidence. By continuously seeing their goals, individuals are constantly reminded of their purpose, keeping their motivation levels high. According to a TD Bank survey[5], individuals who created vision boards were almost twice as confident about achieving their goals than those who chose not to do so. The survey also showed that 82% of small business owners who used vision boards from the inception of their business reported having reached more than half of their goals. A Harvard Business Study[6] found that the 3% of graduates from their MBA who had their goals written down ended up earning ten times as much as the other 97% put together just ten years after graduation.

Visualization is such a powerful concept; the brain sees very little difference between something physically happening and a strongly imagined vision of it. For example, I imagine that I am a marathon finisher again, not just running the race. Because of constant visualization (and meditation on that thought and imagery), I am, more than likely, going to make it happen.

Another powerful brain-vision board connection comes by way of repetition. Generally, when you try something new, the body produces a stress response by way of emitting cortisol and adrenaline. With repeated viewing of the images, your brain is no longer categorizing it as "new," thus decreasing fear-induced responses. This, in turn, now lowers the risk registry in the brain regarding new opportunities; you become more accepting of these opportunities as they come your way.

Creating a vision board is not just an art project; it's a scientifically grounded practice that leverages the power of positive thinking.

ENDNOTES

1. Venus, Claire. How Does a Vision Board Actually Work. March 2024. https://creativelyconscious.substack.com/p/a-vision-board;

2. ibid #1

3. ibid #1

4.Niles, Frank. How to Use Visualization to Achieve Your Goals. June 2011. https://www.huffpost.com/entry/visualization-goals_b_878424;

5. Zimmerman, Eilene. Survey Shows Visualizing Success Works. January 2016. https://www.forbes.com/sites/eilenezimmerman/2016/01/27/survey-shows-visualizing-success-works/?sh=168b7635760b.

6. Acton, Annabel. How To Set Goals. November 2017 https://www.forbes.com/sites/annabelacton/2017/11/03/how-to-set-goals-and-why-you-should-do-it/?sh=73ca7701162d;

Visioneering 101 – The Art of Seeing

Visioneering, the merging of "vision" (the ability to see or imagine a future aspiration) and "engineering" (the practical steps to achieve it), reflects the idea of not only envisioning your future but also designing and building it. It is the process of actively creating and planning for your future by painting a mental picture of your goals and dreams, and then taking intentional actions to bring them to life. Staying focused on your vision and overcoming obstacles is a key component. This strategic mindset encourages maintaining a positive, growth-oriented mindset.

In essence, visioneering is about combining the power of visualization with practical, strategic planning. It goes beyond mere mental ascent of what you want to achieve to deliberately developing a roadmap of the steps and strategies required to reach said aspirations.

Visioneering is effective because it is instrumental in articulating a detailed vision, connects you to your "why," the driving force behind your goals, and ensures that you're not just daydreaming, but thoughtfully planning and executing the necessary steps to manifest your goals.

Key elements of visioneering include:

1. *Defining what you want to achieve*—short, mid- and, long-term goals, aspirations, or dreams. This should cover personal, professional, social, financial, spiritual, and relational goals.

2. *Creating a vividly clear mental image of what that future looks like.* This is where the vision board comes into play. Also visualize accomplishing your new daily routine and practicing good habits.

3. *Breaking down that vision into actionable steps.* This includes setting milestones, deadlines, and creating a roadmap to success (we will further address this in the next chapter).

In short, visioneering requires more than just a pictorial representation of your dreams. It emphasizes the importance of persistent work toward your goals, adjusting along the way to stay on track. It helps you to envision possibilities and outcomes beyond your present reality for:

1. Personal Growth: Designing your ideal life, improving self-discipline, or achieving balance to become the kind of person you desire.

2. Career/Business: Advancing your career, starting a business, or leading a team.

3. *Health and Wellness*: Creating a healthier lifestyle or reaching fitness goals.

4. *Relationships*: Building stronger personal or professional connections.

5. *Financial Success*: Achieving financial freedom or managing wealth.

6. *Social Impact*: Creating change in your community or environment.

At this point, I trust that you are gaining a clear picture of this better life for yourself. Now it's time to put it on paper, starting with a vision board. For some who may not know and a quick reminder for others, a vision board is a visual representation of your goals, dreams, and aspirations. It typically consists of a collage made from images, words, and quotes that represent the things you want to achieve in your life.

The process of creating a vision board involves gathering pictures, magazine cutouts, or printed images that symbolize the things you desire, such as career goals, personal growth, health, relationships, travel, or financial achievements. You then arrange these elements on a board or poster and display it in a prominent location so that you can regularly see it. This constant reminder helps reinforce your focus and intentions. The idea behind a vision board is to make your goals more tangible and clearer by focusing on them regularly.

You can make a vision board in any size or shape, using pictures, words, stickers, or a combination of all of these. You can also write and draw on your board. There are no rules, so you can be as creative as you want. By developing a vision board, you move those fleeting thoughts and ideas into something tangible.

To create this board:

1. **Gather Your Supplies**: Before diving into the creative process, gather materials such as magazines, scissors, glue, and a sturdy cork board or poster paper. Consider using a board that resonates with you, perhaps in your favorite color or texture.

2. **Define Your Focus**: What areas of your life will be focus for your board? Whether it's career, relationships, health, or personal growth,

identifying specific themes will help you create a more targeted and impactful vision board.

3. **Name It**: Having a theme, name or slogan for your board further personalizes your vision. Assigning a name can help set the tone and intention for your vision board, making it more intimate and inspiring. Here are some sample names that can be used as-is or modified to your liking.

- Visionary Voyage
- Pathway to Purpose
- Blueprint for Greatness
- Life Alignment Board
- Imagination Station
- Life & Legacy Map
- Gratitude & Goals
- Forward Focus
- Journey Ahead Board
- The Life I See

- Dream Big Board
- Vision Vibes
- Goal Getter Board
- The Life I'm Becoming
- Next-Level Me
- Wealth & Wins Board
- Elevate & Empower
- Rise & Flourish
- All I Envision
- My Balanced Life Board

4. **Divide and Conquer**: For each category focus you want to put on the board, create a section for it, and label said section.

5. **Select Images and Words**: Peruse magazines or for my tech people, use sites like Pinterest, Bing, and Google for images and words that

resonate with your goals. Be open-minded and choose visuals that evoke positive emotions, even if they don't seem directly related to your goals at first.

6. **Arrange Elements**: Lay out your selected images and words on your board in a way that feels visually appealing and meaningful. Consider the layout and flow to create a harmonious representation of your aspirations. Don't stress or overthink it. JUST LET IT FLOW!

7. **Add Personal Touches**: Incorporate personal items, quotes, or affirmations that hold significance to you. Your vision board should reflect your unique personality and aspirations.

8. **Apply**: Now it's time to finalize your board. Grab the glue or tape and start to fasten your images and words.

9. **Hang It**: When your vision board is ready, hang it in a visible place where you will naturally encounter it throughout the day. Some examples are the bedroom wall or back of the bedroom door, your home office, family room, etc. Whenever you see it, take a minute to engage with it – reflect on what you have declared on your vision board and envision yourself attracting

For my current board, my theme is "Thrive 360: Reflecting a balanced focus on personal and professional growth." Thrive 360 is a powerful theme that symbolizes achieving holistic growth and success in all areas of my life. The concept focuses on thriving in a well-rounded and balanced way—

spiritually, personally, professionally, emotionally, relationally, financially, and socially. Here's a breakdown of what "Thrive 360" represent to me:

Core Themes of Thrive 360

1. Holistic Growth

    o Thriving in every aspect of life—mind, body, business, relationships, career, and spirit.

    o Emphasis on creating a balance that supports long-term well-being and success.

2. All-Encompassing Perspective

    o Viewing life from a 360-degree lens, where no area is neglected.

    o Focusing on interconnectedness, ensuring personal and professional goals complement each other.

3. Empowerment and Resilience

    o Thriving despite challenges by building emotional strength and self-awareness.

    o Achieving goals with confidence and persistence.

4. Sustainability

    o Ensuring growth in a way that is sustainable, avoiding burnout or imbalance.

    o Emphasizing practices that support ongoing development and fulfillment.

The Art of Seeing

To bring my board to life, I included sections and visuals representing:

1. Personal Goals

   o Self-care routines, fitness milestones, or personal hobbies.

   o Visuals: Images of nature, marathon races, books, and art/painting supplies.

2. Professional Aspirations

   o Career growth, leadership roles, and entrepreneurial success.

   o Visuals: Business icons, motivational quotes, or company logos.

3. Relationships

   o Strengthening connections with husband, children, extended family, friends, and community.

   o Visuals: Photos of loved ones, symbols of togetherness, and heart icons.

4. Emotional and Mental Wellness

   o Fostering positivity, gratitude, and inner peace.

   o Visuals: Bible, prayer and meditation images, affirmations, and serene landscapes.

5. Financial Stability and Growth

   o Achieving financial independence and reaching savings/investment goals.

- ○ Visuals: Pictures of stock market, real estate, a mock will for legacy, stacks of money.

6. Adventures and Experiences

- ○ Traveling, learning new skills, and exploring passions.

- ○ Visuals: Pictures of Dubai, Tahiti, family vacation image, cruise ship, passports, and bucket-list items.

Remember, the journey matters as much as the destination! Be adventurous, be unique, be bold, be all the things that will assert integrity of purpose and imaginative vision against the the creatures of the comfort zone and the slaves of ordinary.

Chapter 4

Visioneering 101 – Ambition in Action

Now that you've listed your values, established your "whys," set your goals, and created a vision board, it now to implement phase 2 of the visioneering strategy. If you're anything like the *old* me, you'll set ALL OF THE GOALS to improve all the areas of your life, and then you'll get overwhelmed three weeks in, you'll burn yourself out, and you'll be right back to where you started. The thing some may tend to forget or not realize is that for every goal being set, there are several components and adjustments to be made. For instance, one of my goals is to train for a marathon… yes, complete 26.2 miles of movement (I may or may not be running ☺). Although that's one goal, in reality, there are five MAJOR components to accomplish this:

1. Short runs twice a week and a long run on the weekends
2. Eat healthier
3. Cross training workouts
4. Get proper rest daily
5. Pay for the marathon or raise money through a sponsoring organization

I am reconstructing numerous habits that I've established over many years. **This takes time.** To avoid being overwhelmed and burnt out, set only a few goals at a time.

Let's pressure test the viability of your goal. My preferred method, as with most people, of creating my goals is using SMART method.

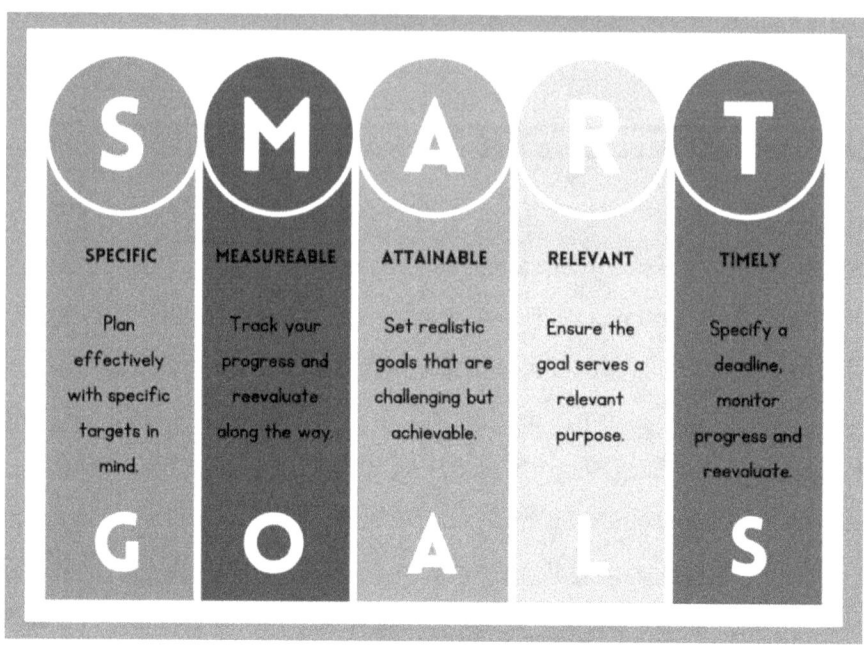

Defining these parameters as they pertain to your goal helps ensure that your objectives are attainable within a certain time frame. This approach reduces generalities and guesswork, sets a clear timeline, and makes it easier to track progress and identify missed milestones.

As beneficial as the S.M.A.R.T. method is, there are some drawbacks that I've experienced using it. First (and biggest for ME), there is a missed opportunity to ask God to show you His plans for you and help you craft them according to _His_ will. S.M.A.R.T goals are said to be achievable and realistic. Achievable according to whom – You? Realistic to whom – the world's standards? With ensuring the goals are realistic, that sometimes removes the God-factor out of your dreaming. If you base it on YOUR natural ability, you're limited. If you lead with God and allow Him to stretch your faith, then what seemed impossible to do now becomes your new starting point!

When you take the God-factor into consideration when setting goals, being SMART about them can be a hindrance to God's best for you. At times, you may set your goals too low or want to accomplish them out of God's sequence and timing. You likely would overestimate what you can do in a year and underestimate what you can do in three years. I like the idea of being specific, and that's my natural default, however, experience has taught me that when you do this, you can become so bogged down with the specifics that you don't see anything more or less than the goal you've created and the path you've decided to take to get there. But what if God wants more for you that you've determined? With a S.M.A.R.T. goals you may not make room for anything greater than the amounts, times, places, and people that you've identified in your goals. There's little to no reliance on God to help you.

My modified version of a S.M.A.R.T. goal now means:

Show Me – ask God to reveal His plan and will for your life

Meaningful – what impact will it make for you and others

Ambitious – does it pull you out your comfort zone

Revolutionary – does it cause you to be an innovative thinker

Trackable – what are your measures of success, timeline, resources

A God-driven goal will take you outside your comfort zone and inside the realm of God's possibilities. Goals like these require you to be courageous and cutting edge. Outside-the-box creativity will become your norm. Allow God to be BIG in your life.

Once you have your goals in mind, put them in writing. I like to use a copy I can physically write as well as use an app to track. For the written portion, I populate all of my information onto this form:

S.M.A.R.T. GOALS WORKSHEET

GOAL Be specific and concise. Include the benchmarks for success.		MY GOAL IS...	✔
		Show Me	S
		Meaningful	M
DURATION Short-term (1-12 months), Mid (1-3years, Long (>3 years)	**LEVEL OF PRIORITY** Essential, Important, Indulgent	Ambitious	A
		Refinable	R
		Trackable	T
PURPOSE Why is the goal relevant? What are the benefits? Who are the beneficiaries?		COMPLETION DATE	
		__ / __ / __	
RISKS What are the challenges to overcome? What resources and skills are needed?			

KEY STEPS				
How will you achieve your goal? What are the actions/tasks and milestones? What are the needed resources?				
Description	Start Date	Completion Date	Completion Date	✔

TRACKING									
Keep a log of your progress.									
Date	Measure	Date	Measure	Date	Measure	Date	Measure	Date	Measure

To download a copy, go to www.castingvision.biz/goals

For me, the best way to monitor my goals is through a goal-tracking app. I prefer ClickUp, as I not only get the goal-tracking app but also access to their productivity platform. The app digitally tracks my targets but also provides a weekly scorecard to double down on my tracking efforts, I also put my goals and milestones in my cell phone calendar to ensure I have a backup system reminding me of what I need to do and when! If you're a wall calendar person, add your actions and milestones on there too! One of the worst things you can do is put in all this work to plan your strategy and then forget about actually executing it.

TIPS:

1. I **HIGHLY** recommend you create a weekly and monthly plan by breaking your goals into daily, weekly, and monthly tasks to stay consistent.
2. Identify skills that will help you achieve your goals and seek opportunities to learn them.
3. Replace unproductive habits with ones that align with your vision,
4. Regularly consult trusted friends, mentors, or professionals for constructive input.

Chapter 5

Faith, Focus and Front Loading

To accomplish anything in life, it's going to take faith, focus, and building yourself up in advance of any challenge that may arise (front loading). The key to being effective in life is to do what is essential to _your_ purpose. You must have the conviction that the effort you're putting in will eventually pay off; a focused and faith-filled mindset helps you push through setbacks and uncertainty. Even when your results aren't immediately visible and the outcome is unclear, your faith in God and in yourself will keep you anchored in confidence and gives you the resolve to keep pressing forward.

Focus, on the other hand, ensures you remain committed and concentrated on your goals. It's all about minimizing distractions (bonus points if you can eliminate them altogether), making the best use of your time, and _consistently_ working on those things that are essential to your purpose. Because you are on borrowed time, you don't have time to do everything that comes to your mind. If you spread your energy out and diffuse it over many things, you'll reduce your impact.

Together, faith provides the inner strength and confidence, while focus keeps you on the right path and moves you forward consistently.

Faith without action leads to stagnation and focus without belief can lead to burnout. One way to guard against stagnation and burnout is to be intentional with your time, talents, and even your thoughts. A powerful tool to boost intentionality is positive affirmations. Repeating empowering statements daily helps to improve confidence and unlock inner strength as you step forward on the path to creating the life you're meant to live. Below are some affirmations to add to your arsenal:

- I believe in myself and my goals.
- I am learning to trust myself to achieve my goals.
- I am 100% committed to making my goals a reality.
- I take action towards my goals every day.
- I know that anything is possible when I take action.
- I am seeing consistent results from my actions.
- I am motivated and energized to achieve my goals.
- Every day, I am closer and closer to achieving my goals.
- I am easily able to find any resources I require to achieve my goals.
- I enjoy taking action to make my goal a reality.
- I start the day knowing what I want to accomplish.
- I use my time wisely and effectively to ensure that I am successful each day.
- Making certain that I am successful each day ensures that I am successful over each month, year, and decade.
- I am worthy of success.
- I am surrounded by people who support my success and love me.
- I persist even when things get difficult.
- I know that failure is only temporary and that I will learn from it.
- I am continuously learning and growing.
- I am open to new opportunities that will help me achieve my goals.
- I take responsibility for my own success.
- I have a strong work ethic and I am dedicated to reaching my goals.
- I am organized and efficient in my pursuit of success.
- I take time each day to visualize myself achieving my goals.

- I am flexible and adaptable, willing to change my plans if necessary.
- I am grateful for all the opportunities and resources available to me.
- I have everything I need within me to achieve my goals.
- God is by my side to help me achieve my goals.
- All my needs are being met as I move towards my goals.
- My success is inevitable, and I am excited to achieve it.
- I am creating my ideal life, one goal at a time.

It's best to write or print them out and read them multiple times throughout the week to help program your subconscious for success. You can also pick out your favorite ones and post them in places where you'll see them frequently throughout your day (I have some on my mirror, refrigerator, computer and even on my phone screen saver). As you're using these affirmations, remember to focus on the feelings behind them – *feel* the excitement and the satisfaction of achievement as you're reading them!

Remember, success is not always linear, and setbacks are an unavoidable part of the journey. Embrace the challenges, learn from them, and keep moving forward. With perseverance, determination, and a supportive mindset, you can overcome these obstacles and reach the goals you've set for yourself.

Chapter 6

Danger Ahead

According to a survey conducted by Forbes Health (2023), approximately 8% of people said their new year's resolution lasted a month, 22% reported two months and 22% reported three months, while 13% reported their commitment to their resolution lasted four months. A mere one percent reported that they stuck to their resolution for the duration of the year. This number is proof positive that creating a goal is not enough.

In today's fast-paced world, staying resolute to your goals is, in the words of my four-year-old daughter, downright trifficult (tricky x difficult). Oppositions are omnipresent, and the inundation of information can overwhelm and swerve your attention from what truly matters to your essential activities. Lack of focus leads to a common problem of drifting away from your goal and losing sight of your objectives.

With goals and associated actions waxing cold as time progresses, one must question the visionary's focus and resolve. When aspirations are deprioritized, passions become deflated, and motivation dwindles. Productivity suffers, opportunities are missed, and personal and professional growth stalls. The disappointment of unfulfilled objectives can end up cementing your feet in the concrete of stagnation, impacting mental well-being and overall satisfaction. The longer this cycle continues, the more daunting it becomes to reorient and regain lost ground.

Yet, it's precisely in overcoming these challenges that you grow, become stronger, and move closer to achieving your goals.

Factors like distractive time wasters (really how much time do you need to be on IG), poisonous perfectionism, and burnout will call your bluff and challenge you to abandon your post and aggressively attack your momentum. Negative self-talk, that little voice in your head that tells you that you can't do it, can also be a big instigator and imposter. If you don't arrest that voice, those thoughts will consume you and live rent-free in your mind.

Fear of failure is yet another divisive tool used to stymie progress. It's normal to proceed with caution when it comes to unfamiliar things, people, and environments. However, allowing fear to paralyze you can prevent you from taking the necessary risks and seizing opportunities that lead to success. To conquer your fear of failure, reimagine how you view failure. Shift your attitude to now see failure as a stepping stone to learning and growth. Embrace the lessons failure offers, so you can use them as fuel to persist on your journey toward reaching your goals.

Procrastination, the mother of all vices, is a silent assassin. As someone who constantly battles with procrastination, I know how easy it can be to get caught up in distractions that slowly descend into something much less productive. If you have ever gotten stuck in a TikTok or X chokehold, then you know exactly what I am talking about here. This is just one form of unproductive busyness that will sneakily steal time and stop you from reaching your goals.

So, what can you do to avoid procrastinating and veering off course?

1. **Break down each task into smaller chunks.** People often procrastinate because they get overwhelmed and don't know where to start—so they just don't start at all. But if you break things down, it will help you work through each step at a more manageable pace.

2. **Minimize distractions as much as possible.** For example, if your goal is to write your book but you are consistently getting distracted by other things while on your laptop, try writing the first draft by hand, or turning your WiFi off while you are writing.

3. **Ensure that you have the right tools to do the task at hand.** For example, because I am training for a marathon, I will need running shoes specially designed for distance running and the proper moisture-wicking clothes, my go-to app, Nike Run Club, reminds me of the activities I need to do for the week, lets me know when to switch my shoes out and gives me training tips.

4. **Remember that ANY progress towards your goals (no matter how small) is still progress.** Be patient with yourself and remember that Rome wasn't built in a day!

Once you get strong enough to fight off procrastination, its hideous twin, lack of support, wants to pop up and run interference. So let's not add to this by trying to be the solo act in an ensemble cast! Attempting to achieve your goals in isolation can be an uphill battle. Surrounding yourself with a supportive network of friends, family, mentors, or like-minded individuals can provide the encouragement and accountability needed to stay motivated. Seek out individuals who share your aspirations or have already accomplished similar goals. Their wisdom, guidance, and shared experiences can help you navigate obstacles and stay focused on your journey.

To win this war of wills, you've got to curate a resilient mindset. Resilience is your capacity to recover from difficulties is the cornerstone of a mindset that allows you to pursue your goals undeterred by the challenges you encounter. To achieve such a mindset, you need to focus on key aspects of your personal growth, such as bolstering your confidence, effectively managing stress, and shifting your perspective on failure. Develop or deepen your practice of healthy mental health habits like regular exercise, proper rest, balanced meals and prayer and meditation.

Chapter 7

Review, Revise, Regroup

Have you ever set a goal and then forgot about it? Or maybe you set a goal and worked on it here and there, making little progress? It's easy to let things slide without any thought but then you get to December and SHAZAM, you realize you didn't accomplish the lofty goals you had planned for the 12-month period. Before you beat yourself up and dumpster dive into despair, just know that you are not alone. I've been there a time or ten! If only there were tools to remind you of the bigger goal and to see what progress was made thus far. Ahhh but there is. WELCOME TO YOUR MID-YEAR CHECK-IN. Halfway through the year (or six months after you've set your goals and developed an action plan) is the PERFECT time to check on your goals and more importantly, track your progress.

For some of you who's had a level of success with accomplishing your goals and didn't employ the check-in method, congratulations! Chance was on your side. Don't expect lightning to strike twice. You must be intentional with tracking your successes. Do not allow pride or stubbornness cause you to circumvent maximum progress and success.

This may be uncharted waters for you but take my word. You don't want to skip this step. I urge you to sit down with those goals you set and revisit them. Your future you will thank you! By regularly assessing your progress, you can make immediate adjustments to ensure you are always progressing in the right direction.

So, it's safe to say one of the biggest reasons you should review your goals is to see your progress. Checking in with your goals doesn't need to be a tedious task. It can be as simple as going down the list of goals you are working on and making sure you are on track. If you aren't on track, it's a great time to figure out why! Identify the barriers or any struggles you are having. That way, you can work on those things now instead of realizing them at the end of the year!

You can also take some time to do a reality check. If some of the goals are too big or not even necessary anymore, you can change things. It's always okay to tweak your goals. Nothing is set in stone!

Finally, a mid-year check-in is a great time to get excited again! Whether in January or June, the commencement of goal setting is filled with excitement, possibilities and motivation. As time goes on, the motivation definitely drops, so a six-month check-in can be the perfect time for a motivation revival.

Take a deep breath! You've got this!

So, you are ready to do a mid-year check-in but don't really know what to do or what to focus on… I got you! Here are the steps for doing a HELPFUL goal review!

1. **Pull up the goals and action plan you developed six months ago**. Hopefully you can readily access they via an app, from your computer, or the form you wrote by hand.
2. **Review your progress**. Go through your milestones one by one. It will be easy to see the progress of some goals (ex. If it was numbers-driven goal like a certain amount saved, weight loss, time spent with family, number of day you worked out). Others will be more

challenging (data may need to be gathered) but just focus on any progress made. I recommend writing out everything you've done so far for the goal. For example, my goal is to train for a marathon so I've been working out three times a week and cutting back on carbs except on run days.

Ask yourself:

- What has changed in my life since I first set this goal?

- Am I prepared to put in the needful effort to achieve my goals?

- What might stop me?

  o Is my level of resourcing (money, time, information, support) adequate?

  o Is a lack of resources holding me back from achieving my goal?

- How will I overcome this?

3. **Review your "why."** I may sound like a broken record at this point ,but I will risk saying it again. Motivation can really decrease as time passes, so it's vital to not only review your progress but it's equally critical to review your "why." Why do you want these goals? Why are you doing all this work? Why are you making such sacrifices? Remind yourself of the reasons you are trying to achieve the goals! If your "why" is no longer obvious, ask yourself if the goal is still

relevant AND one you want to continue to pursue. Sometimes priorities change or desires change. It's okay to pivot!

4. **Fix it or nix it**. If you notice one or two (or more) of your goals are not moving forward, you need to be transparent with yourself. What is not working? Are you lacking the time needed to work on the goals? Is the goal too big? Are you simply not prioritizing it? Or maybe you're not passionate about the goal. Whatever the reasons are, you need to find out immediately so you can either fix the issues or nix the goal. Make a list of the steps you've tried but had little to no success. Whether it was a factor of you not completing the task at hand or something didn't work, detail as much as you can. It may be a tough reality to face, but I am asking you to write down why it failed and what you could change moving forward. A mid-year check-in is all about reflection.

5. **Create a plan for the rest of the year**. Part of figuring out what is not working is regrouping and resetting your path. Designing the action was phase one, walking out said plan was the next step. Then you reviewed , now it's time to push forward on how the next six months will be. In the Fix or Nix phase, you determined what's not working well; if you are to proceed with this goal, now's the time to reset your action plan. For each goal, ask yourself:

- Realistically, is it possible to achieve this goal by the end of the next six months?

- If not, how far can I get towards achieving this goal by the end of the next six months?

- What are all the steps I need to take from here to achieve this?

- What are my next three steps?

- What are the next three after that?

Revisions to the milestones and deadlines of your action plan are needed For example, if your goal is to lose 10 pounds and you've noticed no change in the last 6 months, you need to reset your milestones. They may look something like joining a gym, creating a meal plan, limiting sugary drinks, etc. Then, you will attach deadlines to them. By August 1st I will join a gym. By August 15th, I will create a weekly meal plan for my lunches.

6. **Reward yourself**. Sometimes goal reviews can be a daunting, especially if you haven't made much progress; it can feel like a letdown, which is why many people don't like revisiting their goals after they set them. However, there is **ALWAYS** something to celebrate. Find the small wins and reward yourself. Practice self-compassion and understanding but don't give yourself an excuse to abandon your goals. Yes, you need to be honest with yourself but also be kind to yourself.

7. **Revisit your goals often**. Your goals need to be kept warm and alive. Read through your goals regularly – at least once a week. Try to do something toward your goals every day. Spend some time every week writing in your goal book.

Lists are a powerful means of reflection. Try listing:

- What I've accomplished so far is…

- New possibilities are…

- Things that are blocking me from moving forward are…

- My advice to myself is…

- The positive outcomes I see for the future are…

I think it may be useful to do a quick daily journal, a biweekly review meeting with your mentor, or a monthly catch-up with an accountability partner. A bit intense, you betcha. Yet, if you are desperate enough for change, do what you haven't done before, which is allowing your trusted circle to be knee deep in your business. You might be surprised at how much more you can achieve when others are keeping a close eye on your progress.

Once the six months have passed, **conduct a year-end / 12-month review**. Answer the following questions:

- What has changed for you? With you? For your household? For your marriage? For your relationships?
- What has remained the same?
- List your top three goals you accomplished.
- List your top three goals that are still progressing.
- List your top three goals which need to change.
- Do your investments (include how you invest your time and talent) reflect your values?
- How effective has your marketing and promotional efforts been? Analyze the performance of your content marketing strategy (search ads, social media, email campaigsixns, vlog and blog posts, etc.)
- Reflect on the conversations you've been having with potential clients in the last six months. Are you effectively nurturing your leads?
- Identify opportunities to grow you circle (joining groups like Chamber of Commerce, industry focused networks,

etc), cultivate collaborations, or create strategic partnerships.

- How are your products or services meeting customer needs and expectations? Ask for feedback from your customers to assess customer satisfaction levels. What's working well? What needs to be improved?

- What trends or changes in the industry over the past 12 months had an impact your business?

- How effective have you been in managing your mindset? What can be improved?

- How effective have you been in managing your time? What shifts need to happen for your time to be more productive?

- How effective have you been in managing your energy? What do you need to change to feel more energized on a daily basis?

CONGRATULATIONS! YOU HAVE COMPLETED YOUR 12-MONTH REVIEW. TAKE A BOW!

Keep your goals and reviews in one place. I am a HUGE fan of apps (as you may have figured out by now) and journaling. Yes I double down on the same activities but it works for me! Journaling is for daily activities and the app is for my milestone tracking. It keeps me organized and helps me to easily locate, within seconds, my progress.

Don't compare yourself with ANYONE! It's great to admire and read about other people's success but don't get so caught up in their journey that you begin to compare and contrast your path and progress with theirs. It's neither healthy nor the best use of your time. IT'S YOUR RACE, AT YOUR PACE!

You are one-of-one, therefore you will have a story that's all your own. Different journey, different plan, different support, different results. It's okay if you take longer to achieve something.

Lastly, set a time limit. As previously stated, this does not need to be a tedious task. Depending on how many goals you set, you may need more time, but start by setting aside 30-45 minutes.

TIPS

- You are not defined by your goal progress! Always do your best but remember that ticking off a goal is not proof of your worth.

- You're the only person who can achieve your goals. If you decide to put in the effort or not, it is ultimately up to you and you only.

- We all have bad days. Life, business, relationships are all unpredictable and sometimes chaotic. As the adage goes, "Life can sometimes get in the way of living." Feel all the feels then FORGIVE YOURSELF. Once that time is over, pick yourself back up and keep pressing forward with the plan. Don't let a bad day or even a trying week derail your whole month or even year!

BIOGRAPHY

*WIFE, MOTHER, ENTREPRENEUR, AND AUTHOR,
CHARITY IS PASSIONATE ABOUT HELPING PEOPLE
REALIZE AND REACH THEIR GREATEST POTENTIAL.*

 Charity is a dynamic teacher who has a gifted ability to communicate with clarity, simplicity, revelation, and passion. She pulls from her experiences and uses humor to help keep her audience actively engaged, entertained, and edified. She has conducted trainings, seminars, workshops, and taught classes in the public and private sector.

As a communicator, she has authored books to help people maximize living, with the latest being 21-Day Spending Detox. She holds a B.A. in Psychology and an A.A. in French from Indiana University Northwest. In 2009, she also graduated from the Joseph Business School. Charity's entrepreneurial gifts manifested as she started her own publishing company, Scribe Publications as well as an merchandising company, Grace Gear.

Charity is the wife of Gary Morris. To their beautiful union, they have four amazing children and reside in Georgia.

If you would like to book Charity to speak at your conference, service, or event, please email booking@charitymorris.com